A Promise Kept At Christmas

Christmas Eve Service

Robert G. McCreight

CSS Publishing Company, Inc.
Lima, Ohio

A PROMISE KEPT AT CHRISTMAS

0-7880-0096-9

Christmas is a time for families. Distances and schedules are overcome so the family can share a sacred time together — recalling memories and creating new ones. The church, too, gathers across the miles to remember and to celebrate.

This reality often puts the minister and his or her family in conflict. When the church family gathers on Christmas Eve, the pastor is expected to be there in leadership. Personal family plans are made around the parish activities.

This Christmas Eve worship service is dedicated to my wife, Marianne, who knows well the tension between church expectations and family plans.

Christmas Eve Candlelight Service

The Order Of Worship

We approach the worship of God this evening with a hushed awareness of Christ's presence in our midst. God again breaks through the calm and darkness to reveal himself to us in the stillness of our hearts. Let the praises of your heart and the songs of your voice be "joyful yet restrained" that we might be sensitive to the quiet indwelling of his Spirit.

Organ And Piano Prelude
"And He Shall Feed His Flock"   Handel

Introit
"Let All Mortal Flesh Keep Silence"   The Chancel Choir

The Call To Worship

Leader: The darkness can be a place of fear and of shame. But it can also be the opportunity to find life and hope.

People: **From the busy walkways of life we stumble through the dark, seeking to find a light that might lead us back onto the path of faith.**

Leader: On this sacred night, when the darkness haunts so many lives with remorse and despair, we gather together in the house of the Lord to pray for light. Light for ourselves, and light for all who are living in darkness.

People: **Remembering the birth of our Lord and Savior, Jesus Christ, may we be brought by the light through our darkness into the joy of new life and hope.**

5

The Lighting Of The Advent Candles

Christmas Eve is precious in the eyes of the Lord and in our traditions as well. It is a time when we put aside resentments and falsehood for at least one brief moment, and reflect upon the purity and promise of the baby of Bethlehem who became King of the Universe. We join with Christians this night all over the world to celebrate his coming into the world and his abiding presence in our lives.

Hear the words of this truth found in scripture:

For a child has been born for us, a son given to us;
authority rests upon his shoulders. (Isaiah 9:6)

Glory to God in the highest heaven and on earth peace
among those whom he favors! (Luke 2:14)

(The first four candles are lit.) Tonight as we re-light the four candles of Advent, we pause once again to consider the blessings we have anticipated in the past: hope, peace, love, and joy. Tonight we lift up the gift of God which is the reality of those blessings — our Lord Jesus Christ. He is the greatest gift. He makes all other blessings possible.

(Light the center Christ-candle.) As I light this Christmas Eve candle, I pray that Christ may find you in some wonderful way, and grant you those blessings which you need most. Amen.

A Promise Kept At Christmas

A dramatic reading using portions of scripture to tell why and how God had demonstrated his marvelous love. At certain times the congregation is requested to be participants, as marked in the bulletin. (Please remain seated for the singing of the hymns.)

The Light Of God In Creation And Covenant

Genesis 1:1-5; Jeremiah 33:25-26;
Psalm 27:1; Proverbs 4:18-19

6

The Failure Of God's People To Live By The Light .

Isaiah 59:9-14; Micah 7:8-9

The Expectation Of God's Messiah

Isaiah 59:15b-17, 20-21; Psalm 130:5-6

The Hymn
"Watchman, Tell Us Of The Night"

A Duet
"Lo, How A Rose E'er Blooming"

Zechariah 14:6-7; Isaiah 60:19-20, 1-4a;
Isaiah 49:6; Acts 26:18

The Choral Anthem
"The Race That Long In Darkness Pined"

The Incarnation Of God's Light

Luke 1:26-33; John 1:6-9, 15;
Isaiah 9:2-3, 6-7; John 1:5

A Solo
"O Holy Night"

Luke 2:8-14

The Choral Anthem
"In Silent Night"   Southall

The Hymn
"Silent Night! Holy Night!" *(verses 1, 3 and 4)*

The Hymn
"There's A Song In The Air!" *(verses 1, 3 and 4)*

Hebrews 1:1-3; 2 Timothy 1:9-10

7

Jesus' Ministry And The Implications For Our Life Today

John 12:46, 8:12, 9:5, 12:35-36;
Ephesians 5:8-11; Romans 13:12-13a

The Hymn
"Break Forth, O Living Light Of God" *(verses 1, 4 and 5)*

The Benediction
Colossians 1:11-14

Our Response To The Light Of The World
Our offering this evening will be taken in support of . . .

The Offertory Prayer *(Unison)*
All glory to you, O God, who has brought light into darkness and hope into the world. You have made this a most holy night, and ordained it to shine with the brightness of the true light which has come to save mankind. As we embrace the mysteries of your love for us, may we also come to the fullness of your joy and your peace; through your Son, Jesus Christ, we pray. Amen.

The Offertory
Selected music

The Closing Hymn
"Go, Tell It On The Mountain" *(Please stand)*

The Benediction *(Unison)*
Now, Lord, you have kept your promise, and you may let your servant go in peace. With my own eyes I have seen your salvation, which you have prepared in the presence of all peoples; a light to reveal your will to the Gentiles and bring glory to your people Israel. Amen.

A Choral Response
"Peace On Earth"

The Postlude
Selected music

The Service In Detail

The following script and order of service is ready to use in your congregation as you celebrate the birth of Jesus Christ on this sacred Christian holiday. Directions are provided to direct you in how to effectively utilize the program. However, the availability of special and congregational music, as well as the particular uniqueness of your worship facility, may suggest or require certain modifications. You should feel free to adapt the service to best fit your circumstances.

Scripture passages are taken from the *New Revised Standard Version of the Bible*. You may prefer to use another translation, and may substitute the wording as you prefer.

The script is designed to be read by two or more persons. It alternates between passages of scripture and original commentary. People reading from a pulpit and a lectern would be an appropriate way to deliver this program.

If possible, it is most appropriate to begin the service with the sanctuary only dimly-lit. As the service progresses, the amount of light may be decreased and then increased to underscore the theme of God bringing the Light of our salvation into the world. Candelabra may also be used to add a classic touch visually representing to the congregation that the Light of God's messiah is coming into our lives. (The script indicates those points where the amount of light should be changed. Stage directions for levels of light range from a low of one to a high of ten. The service begins with the sanctuary lights set at a level of "3.")

A Promise Kept At Christmas
Genesis 1:1-15

In the beginning, when God created the heavens and the earth, the earth was a formless void and darkness covered the face of the deep, while a wind from God swept over the face of the waters. Then God said, "Let there be light"; and

9

there was light. And God saw that the light was good; and God separated the light from the darkness. God called the light Day, and the darkness he called Night. And there was evening and there was morning, the first day.

Narrator: Time began as God brought light into a vast sea of darkness. In measured increments of time God marked the day and the night by an alteration of light and darkness. The coming of light into the darkness was the original manifestation of the activity of God, and represents for all time thereafter the divine operation of God. The alternation of light and darkness reveals the nature of God's work — to bring order where formerly there was chaos.

God went on to create other parts of the world, and give to each one its name. He created humankind in his own image, and he breathed into him the breath of life. With the people of Israel he made a covenant that he would be their God, and they would be his people. By the light of this covenant he brought order to their fragmented life, and provided for their historical destiny as they sought to live in faithfulness.

(Light the first candle.)

Jeremiah 33:25-26
Thus says the Lord: Only if I had not established my covenant with day and night and the ordinances of heaven and earth, would I reject the offspring of Jacob and of my servant David and not choose any of his descendants as rulers over the offspring of Abraham, Isaac, and Jacob. For I will restore their fortunes, and will have mercy upon them.

Narrator: Through the covenant God made with the people of Israel each successive generation received the promise of salvation. They took assurance in God's protective custody.

Psalm 27:1
The Lord is my light and my salvation; whom shall I fear? The Lord is the stronghold of my life; of whom shall I be afraid?

Narrator: The people of Israel began to think of their faithful obedience to God's ways as walking in the light, whereas those who rebelled against God ignoring his laws were like those who chose to live in darkness.

Proverbs 4:18-19
The path of the righteous is like the light of dawn, which shines brighter and brighter until full day. The way of the wicked is like deep darkness; they do not know what they stumble over.

Reduce The Sanctuary Lights To The Level Of ONE.

Narrator: The years of Israel's life in covenant with God became decades, and then centuries. Each new generation grew farther from the promises of the covenant — both in time and in practice. They claimed to be the people of light, but many turned their backs on God and his righteousness, living as do those possessed by wickedness and sin. The darkness that existed before the time of creation seemed to represent the oppression and unwholesomeness of the people of Israel who had cut themselves off from God.

Isaiah 59:9-14
Therefore justice is far from us, and righteousness does not reach for us; we wait for light, and lo! there is darkness; and for brightness, but we walk in gloom. We grope like the blind along a wall, groping like those who have no eyes; we stumble at noon as in the twilight, among the vigorous as though we were dead. We all growl like bears; like doves we moan mournfully. We wait for justice, but there is none; for salvation, but it is far from us. For our transgressions before you are many, and our sins testify against us. Our transgressions indeed are with us, and we know our iniquities: transgressing, and denying the Lord, and turning away from following our God, talking oppression and revolt, conceiving lying words and uttering them from the heart. Justice is turned

back, and righteousness stands at a distance; for truth stumbles in the public square, and uprightness cannot enter.

Narrator: God continued to watch over Israel as one generation after another broke the covenant. He felt a great anger toward them for their waywardness. And he also knew a great compassion for them, longing for their faithfulness and a return to his ways of righteousness. He sent prophets like Isaiah and Jeremiah, like Amos and Micah, to convict them of their sin and plead with them to come back to the hope of their salvation.

Through the voice of one like Micah, some of the people heard God's call to put off their wicked and faithless ways to return to a life of obedience and love. They acknowledged their sin, and through long years of patient waiting, trusted God to redeem the people whom he loved.

Micah 7:8-9

Do not rejoice over me, O my enemy; when I fall, I shall rise; when I sit in darkness, the Lord will be a light to me. I must bear the indignation of the Lord, because I have sinned against him, until he takes my side and executes judgment for me. He will bring me out to the light; I shall see his vindication.

(Light the second candle.)

Narrator: As the faint spark of hope flickered in the hearts of the faithful, the people looked to the time when God would punish them no longer, but send a messiah to restore the nation.

(Organ music begins at this point, playing softly one verse of "O Come, O Come Emmanuel.")

Narrator: The people of Israel who so much needed to be delivered from the bondage and oppression of their sin prayed for a new dawn which would draw back the shadow of night.

Isaiah 59:15b-17, 20-21

The Lord saw it, and it displeased him that there was no justice. He saw that there was no one, and was appalled that there was no one to intervene; so his own arm brought him victory, and his righteousness upheld him. He put on righteousness like a breastplate, and a helmet of salvation on his head; he put on garments of vengeance for clothing, and wrapped himself in fury as in a mantle.

And he will come to Zion as Redeemer, to those in Jacob who turn from transgression, says the Lord. And as for me, this is my covenant with them, says the Lord: my spirit that is upon you, and my words that I have put in your mouth, shall not depart out of your mouth, or out of the mouths of your children, or out of the mouths of your children's children, says the Lord, from now on and forever.

(Light the third candle.)

Narrator: The hope and expectations of the people grew, and could not be held back.

Psalm 130:5-6

I wait for the Lord, my soul waits, and in his word I hope; my soul waits for the Lord more than those who watch for the morning, more than those who watch for the morning.

Congregational Hymn "Watchman, Tell Us Of The Night"

Narrator: Through years of long waiting in the darkness of sin the people of Israel clung to the promise of God's returning light. They did not know when or how, but they fueled their faith with hope.

Duet "Lo, How A Rose E'er Blooming"

Narrator: Through the words of the prophets Israel gradually awakened to the understanding that the coming of the light of salvation would be more than a flaring burst of light which fills the skies and then disappears. It would be an eternal light that would change the course of history forevermore.

Zechariah 14:6-7
On that day there shall not be either cold or frost. And there shall be continuous day (it is known to the Lord), not day and not night, for at evening time there shall be light.

Isaiah 60:19-20, 1-4a
The sun shall no longer be your light by day, nor for brightness shall the moon give light to you by night; but the Lord will be your everlasting light, and your God will be your glory. Your sun shall no more go down, or your moon withdraw itself; for the Lord will be your everlasting light, and your days of mourning shall be ended.

Arise, shine; for your light has come, and the glory of the Lord has risen upon you. For darkness shall cover the earth, and thick darkness the peoples; but the Lord will arise upon you, and his glory will appear over you. Nations shall come to your light, and kings to the brightness of your dawn. Lift up your eyes and look around; they all gather together, they come to you.

(Light the fourth candle.)

Narrator: Not only was Israel to be the recipient of God's salvation, but she was to be the beacon of the light of salvation to the Gentile world living in darkness.

Isaiah 49:6
[The Lord said to me] he says, "It is too light a thing that you should be my servant to raise up the tribes of Jacob and to restore the survivors of Israel; I will give you as a light to the nations, that my salvation may reach to the end of the earth."

Bring The Sanctuary Lights Up To The Level Of FOUR.

Acts 26:18

[You are] To open their eyes so that they may turn from darkness to light and from the power of Satan to God, so that they may receive forgiveness of sins and a place among those who are sanctified by faith in me.

Choral Anthem "The Race That Long In Darkness Pined" *(verses 1, 2, and 5)*

Narrator: At last the time had come for the fullness of God to be revealed. It came quietly at first — to a young girl to whom an angel of the Lord appeared.

Luke 1:26-33

In the sixth month the angel Gabriel was sent by God to a town in Galilee called Nazareth, to a virgin engaged to a man whose name was Joseph, of the house of David. The virgin's name was Mary. And he came to her and said, "Greetings, favored one! The Lord is with you."

But she was much perplexed by his words and pondered what sort of greeting this might be. The angel said to her, "Do not be afraid, Mary, for you have found favor with God. And now, you will conceive in your womb and bear a son, and you will name him Jesus. He will be great, and will be called the Son of the Most High, and the Lord God will give to him the throne of his ancestor David. He will reign over the house of Jacob forever, and of his kingdom there will be no end."

Narrator: Soon all the world would be told of the Messiah's coming.

John 1:6-9, 15

There was a man sent from God, whose name was John. He came as a witness to testify to the light, so that all might believe through him. He himself was not the light, but he came to testify to the light. The true light, which enlightens everyone, was coming into the world. John cried out, "This was he of whom I said, 'He who comes after me ranks ahead of me because he was before me.' "

Isaiah 9:2-3, 6-7

The people who walked in darkness have seen a great light; those who lived in a land of deep darkness — on them light has shined. You have multiplied the nation, you have increased its joy; they rejoice before you as with joy at the harvest, as people exult when dividing plunder. For a child has been born for us, a son given to us; authority rests upon his shoulders; and he is named Wonderful Counselor, Mighty God, Everlasting Father, Prince of Peace. His authority shall grow continually and there shall be endless peace for the throne of David and his kingdom. He will establish and uphold it with justice and with righteousness from this time onward and forevermore. The zeal of the Lord of hosts will do this.

Raise The Sanctuary Lights To Level SIX.

John 1:5

The light shines in the darkness, and the darkness did not overcome it.

Narrator: The light which John the Baptist spoke about pierced the darkness and brought the dawning of a new day to the children of God. It came in human form in a remote corner of the world, in a small Judean town called Bethlehem. There a peasant mother gave birth to a boy whom she was told to name Jesus, because he would save the people from their sin.

(Light the fifth candle.)

Solo "O Holy Night"

Narrator: A Galilean carpenter, a newborn child, some nearby shepherds were the unrehearsed actors in God's drama that night. And while the story of salvation was being played out in that Bethlehem stable, all the hosts of heaven were jubilant with the news of the birth of God's Son.

Luke 2:8-14

In that region there were shepherds living in the fields, keeping watch over their flock by night. Then an angel of the

16

Lord stood before them, and the glory of the Lord shone around them, and they were terrified. But the angel said to them, "Do not be afraid; for see — I am bringing you good news of great joy for all the people: to you is born this day in the city of David a Savior, who will be the Messiah, the Lord. This will be a sign for you: you will find a child wrapped in bands of cloth and lying in a manger." And suddenly there was with the angel a multitude of the heavenly host, praising God and saying, "Glory to God in the highest heaven, and on earth peace among those whom he favors!"

Choral Anthem "In Silent Night"

Narrator: The heavens declared the glory of God that night while God's newborn son slept quietly on a manger bed of straw.

(Light the sixth candle.)

Congregational Hymn "Silent Night! Holy Night!"

Narrator: This was more than the birth of a child. It was the coming of God's Son to bring a reign of peace where there was hatred and alienation. Descended from the family of David, this child is the King of Righteousness.

Raise The Sanctuary Lights To The Level Of EIGHT.

Congregational Hymn "There's A Song In The Air!"

Narrator: Jesus was recognized as the fulfillment of God's promise to redeem all people and complete all creation. In him God had done this!

Hebrews 1:1-3
Long ago God spoke to our ancestors in many and various ways by the prophets, but in these last days he has spoken

to us by a Son, whom he appointed heir of all things, through whom he also created the worlds. He is the reflection of God's glory and the exact imprint of God's very being, and he sustains all things by his powerful word. When he had made purification for sins, he sat down at the right hand of the Majesty on high.

2 Timothy 1:9-10
This means understanding that the law is laid down not for the innocent but for the lawless and disobedient, for the godless and sinful, for the unholy and profane, for those who kill their father or mother, for murderers, fornicators, sodomites, slave traders, liars, perjurers, and whatever else is contrary to the sound teaching.

Narrator: As Jesus grew into manhood his life among the people of Israel reflected the vision which God had given him to proclaim. His teaching and healing brought comfort to the afflicted and a blessing to those who followed him. His message of truth was challenging yet simple: "Accept the forgiveness of your sin in the name of the One who sent me."

(Light the seventh candle.)

John 12:46
I have come as light into the world, so that everyone who believes in me should not remain in the darkness.

John 8:12
Again Jesus spoke to them saying, "I am the light of the world. Whoever follows me will never walk in darkness but will have the light of life."

John 9:5
"As long as I am in the world, I am the light of the world."

18

John 12:35-36

Jesus said to them, "The light is with you for a little longer. Walk while you have the light, so that the darkness may not overtake you. If you walk in the darkness, you know where you are going. While you have the light, believe in the light, so that you may become children of light.

Raise The Sanctuary Lights To The Full Level Of TEN.

Narrator: All of us who come after the time of Christ have the beacon of his words as a guide to light the path of our daily living. We who believe in him and follow his ways of peace and love join with the saints through the ages whom God has made to be his family in faith.

Ephesians 5:8-11

For once you were darkness, but now in the Lord you are light. Live as children of light — for the fruit of the light is found in all that is good and right and true. Try to find out what is pleasing to the Lord. Take no part in the unfruitful works of darkness, but instead expose them.

Romans 13:12-13a

The night is far gone, the day is near. Let us then lay aside the works of darkness and put on the armor of light; let us live honorably as in the day.

Congregational Hymn "Break Forth, O Living Light Of God" *(verses 1, 4 and 5)*

Benediction: Colossians 1:11-14

May you be made strong with all the strength that comes from his glorious power, and may you be prepared to endure everything with patience, while joyfully giving thanks to the Father, who has enabled you to share in the inheritance of the saints in light. He has rescued us from the power of darkness and transferred us into the kingdom of his beloved Son, in whom we have redemption, the forgiveness of sins.